dinner recipes cookbook is a collection of simple and delicious meal ideas that can be quickly and easily prepared by home cooks of any skill level. These cookbooks typically include a variety of recipes, ranging from classic comfort foods to international cuisine, all with easy-to-follow instructions and minimal ingredients.

The recipes in an easy dinner recipes cookbook are designed to make meal planning and preparation a breeze, with minimal time and effort required. Many of the recipes can be made in under 30 minutes, making them perfect for busy weeknights or last-minute dinners.

These cookbooks often include helpful tips and tricks for meal planning and preparation, as well as suggestions for ingredient substitutions and variations to accommodate different dietary needs or preferences. They may also include suggestions for pairing dishes with sides or drinks to create a complete meal.

Whether you're a beginner cook looking for simple meal ideas or a seasoned pro looking for new inspiration, an easy dinner recipes cookbook is a great resource for anyone looking to simplify their dinner routine without sacrificing flavor or variety.

Pasta With Roasted Tomatoes And Garlic

Ingredients

1 tablespoon kosher salt
8 ounces uncooked spaghetti
¼ cup extra-virgin olive oil, divided
2 pints multicolored cherry tomatoes
4 garlic cloves, thinly sliced
½ teaspoon kosher salt
¼ teaspoon freshly ground black pepper
2 ounces Parmigiano-Reggiano cheese, shaved
¼ cup small basil leaves

Turn a regular pasta dinner into something special with this delicious and healthy dish of pasta with roasted tomatoes and garlic. The combination of colors, flavors, and textures will make it an appealing meal for kids.

To make this dish, you'll need the following ingredients: 1 tablespoon kosher salt, 8 ounces uncooked spaghetti, ¼ cup extra-virgin olive oil (divided), 2 pints multicolored cherry tomatoes, 4 garlic cloves (thinly sliced), ½ teaspoon kosher salt, ¼ teaspoon freshly ground black pepper, 2 ounces Parmigiano-Reggiano cheese (shaved), and ¼ cup small basil leaves.

To start, preheat the oven to 425°F. Place the tomatoes in a single layer on a baking sheet and sprinkle with 1 tablespoon of olive oil, the sliced garlic, ½ teaspoon kosher salt, and ¼ teaspoon freshly ground black pepper. Roast for 25 minutes until the tomatoes are lightly charred and beginning to burst open.

While the tomatoes are roasting, bring a large pot of salted water to a boil and cook the spaghetti according to package directions.

When the pasta is cooked, drain it and add the remaining olive oil. Mix in the roasted tomatoes and garlic, Parmigiano-Reggiano cheese, and fresh basil leaves. Serve hot or at room temperature for an easy and delicious meal that the kids will love. Enjoy!

Lasagna

This vegetarian lasagna is a healthy and delicious meal that kids of all ages will enjoy! It's packed with nutritious vegetables, savory tomato sauce, and creamy white sauce. To make this dish, start by preheating your oven to 180°C/Gas Mark 4.

Next, prepare the vegetables: cut the red peppers into large chunks and slice the aubergines into ½ cm thick slices. Heat 8 tablespoons of olive oil in a large frying pan over medium heat and add the red pepper chunks and aubergine slices. Cook for 8-10 minutes until they are lightly browned.

In another pan, add 1 tablespoon of olive oil over medium heat and sauté the onions and garlic until soft. Add the carrot and tomato purée and cook for a few minutes. Pour in the wine and allow it to reduce by half before adding the canned tomatoes. Simmer for 20 minutes until you have a thick sauce. Finally, add the basil leaves and season with salt and pepper.

To make the white sauce, melt the butter in a pan over low heat. Add the flour and stir together until there are no lumps. Gradually add in the milk, stirring constantly until it forms a smooth sauce.

Now you're ready to assemble your vegetarian lasagna! Grease an oven-proof dish with olive oil and begin layering with lasagne sheets, vegetables, tomato sauce, white sauce, mozzarella cheese, and cherry tomatoes. Repeat until you have used all the ingredients and top with extra mozzarella cheese. Bake in the preheated oven for 30 minutes, or until golden brown on top.

This vegetarian lasagna is an easy-to-make dish that kids will love! The vegetables are full of healthy vitamins and minerals, while the tomato and white sauces add a wonderful depth of flavor. Serve it up with a side salad for a complete vegetarian meal that's sure to satisfy even the pickiest eaters. Bon appétit!

Spelt Spaghetti

Ingredients

2 cups spelt flour (whole grain spelt or light flour, sifted or 630)
1/2 cup warm water (plus more if needed)
2 large eggs (optional)

Instructions:

In a large mixing bowl, combine the spelt flour and a pinch of salt (if desired). Make a well in the center of the flour.

If using eggs, crack them into the well and whisk them together with a fork. If not, simply add the warm water to the well.

Use a fork or your hands to gradually mix the flour into the liquid until a shaggy dough forms. If the dough seems too dry, add more warm water a tablespoon at a time until it comes together.

Turn the dough out onto a lightly floured surface and knead it for 5-10 minutes until it becomes smooth and elastic.

Cover the dough with a damp cloth and let it rest at room temperature for at least 30 minutes.

After the dough has rested, divide it into four equal portions. Use a pasta machine or rolling pin to roll each portion of dough into thin sheets.

If using a pasta machine, gradually decrease the thickness setting until you reach your desired thickness. If rolling by hand, roll the dough as thin as possible.

Use a spaghetti cutter attachment or a sharp knife to cut the spaghetti into desired length.

Cook the spaghetti in a pot of boiling salted water for 2-4 minutes or until al dente.

Serve the Spelt Spaghetti with your favorite sauce, grated cheese, or fresh herbs. Enjoy!

Lemon Pasta

Ingredients

8 oz. package pasta (any long noodle)
2 - 3 tablespoons vegan butter or olive oil.
3 garlic cloves, minced.
1/4 teaspoon red pepper flakes, or to taste.
2 - 3 lemons (about 1/4 - 1/2 cup), juice of and some zest.
1/4 cup parsley, chopped.
salt & pepper, to taste.

If you're looking for a healthy and delicious pasta dish, this vegan Lemon Pasta is the perfect recipe for you. It's quick and easy to prepare, using simple ingredients like vegan butter or olive oil, minced garlic, red pepper flakes, lemons (juice of and zest), parsley, salt & pepper.

This dish is healthy, flavorful, and sure to impress!

To begin, cook the pasta according to the package instructions. Meanwhile, heat a large skillet over medium heat. Add in vegan butter or olive oil, garlic and red pepper flakes. Cook until fragrant and the garlic has softened slightly (about 1 minute). Stir in the lemon juice and zest and cook for an additional minute.

Drain the cooked pasta and add it to the skillet. Add in parsley, salt & pepper to taste, stirring until combined. Serve the lemon pasta warm with extra red pepper flakes, if desired. Enjoy!

Crispy Black Bean And Sweet Potato Tacos

Ingredients
8-10 tortillas (see notes)
2 14 oz can black beans, drained.
2 sweet potatoes, diced (skin on or peeled)
1 Tablespoon oil.
1/2 teaspoon (each) cumin, paprika, chili powder.
1/2 teaspoon garlic powder.
salt to taste.

These vegetarian black bean and sweet potato tacos are an easy, healthy, and delicious way to get your kids eating vegetarian! They can be made in under 30 minutes with very few ingredients - perfect for busy nights. To prepare, simply heat up the oil in a large skillet over medium-high heat. Add in the diced sweet potatoes and season with cumin, paprika, chili powder, garlic powder and salt. Cook until the potatoes are soft (about 10 minutes). Then add in the drained black beans and cook for another 2-3 minutes until everything is heated through.

To assemble the tacos grab 8-10 tortillas (or however many you like) spread some of the mixture on each taco shell then top with your favorite toppings like shredded cheese, tomatoes, lettuce, or salsa. Enjoy!

These vegetarian tacos are a great way to get your kids eating healthier and trying new vegetarian recipes. They're easy to make, full of flavor, and customizable with whatever toppings you have on hand. Give these vegetarian black bean and sweet potato tacos a try for your next vegetarian dinner! Your family will love them.

Roasted Black Bean Burger

Ingredients

1½ red onions.
200 g mixed mushrooms.
100 g rye bread.
ground coriander.
1 x 400 g tin of black beans.
40 g mature Cheddar cheese.
4 soft rolls.
100 g ripe cherry tomatoes.

Instructions

Preheat the oven to 200°C (180°C fan) / 400°F / Gas Mark 6. Line a baking sheet with parchment paper.

Chop the red onions and mushrooms into small pieces and roast them on the prepared baking sheet for 10-15 minutes or until they are soft and lightly browned.

Cut the rye bread into small cubes and place in a large bowl.

Drain and rinse the black beans and add them to the bowl with the bread cubes.

Grate the Cheddar cheese and add it to the bowl with the bread and beans.

Add the roasted onions and mushrooms to the bowl, along with 2 teaspoons of ground coriander.

Mash the mixture together using a fork or potato masher, until it forms a sticky, cohesive mixture.

Divide the mixture into 4 portions and form each portion into a patty.

Place the patties on the prepared baking sheet and bake in the preheated oven for 15-20 minutes, or until they are firm and crispy.

While the burgers are baking, slice the soft rolls and halve the cherry tomatoes.

Once the burgers are cooked, assemble the sandwiches by placing a patty in each roll and topping with cherry tomato slices. Serve immediately. Enjoy!

Chicken Tacos

Ingredients

¼ cup olive oil.
2 medium yellow onions, finely chopped.
2 bell peppers (any color), finely chopped.
4 cloves garlic, finely chopped.
2 pounds ground chicken (not extra-lean all breast meat)
1 tablespoon paprika.
2 teaspoons ancho chili powder.
1½ teaspoons ground cumin.

Preparing chicken tacos is a healthy and easy dinner option that kids will love. To make them, begin by heating ¼ cup of olive oil in a large skillet over medium-high heat. Add in chopped onions and bell peppers, as well as the minced garlic, stirring everything until it's lightly browned and fragrant.

Then, add in the ground chicken, breaking it up with a spoon as you stir. Once the chicken is cooked through, sprinkle in paprika, ancho chili powder and cumin. Stir everything to combine and let it cook for 3-4 minutes until all of the flavors have melded together.

Once done, serve your chicken tacos with tortillas, your favorite toppings and a side dish. Enjoy!

This is an easy yet tasty way to whip up a healthy dinner for the kids!

By following these easy steps, you can have a delicious batch of chicken tacos ready in no time. Not only are they healthy and delicious, but your kids will love them too! Try it out today for a quick and tasty dinner option.

Enjoy!

Italian Chicken Skillet

Looking for delicious chicken recipes that are easy and fast to make? Look no further! This delicious Italian Chicken Skillet with Sun-Dried Tomatoes is the perfect dish for busy weeknights. Made with delicious seasonings like rosemary, garlic, onion, sun dried tomatoes and spinach this one-pan meal will be a hit in your household. Plus, you can make it dairy-free by swapping out the heavy cream for a can of coconut cream or homemade cashew cream and topping with nutritional yeast instead of cheese. Ready in under 30 minutes, this delicious Italian Chicken Skillet with Sun Dried Tomatoes will become a regular at your dinner table! Enjoy!

This delicious Italian Chicken Skillet with Sun-Dried Tomatoes is the perfect weeknight dinner! With delicious seasonings like rosemary, garlic, onion, sun dried tomatoes and spinach this easy one-pan meal comes together in under 30 minutes. Make it dairy-free by swapping out the heavy cream for a can of coconut cream or homemade cashew cream and topping with nutritional yeast instead of cheese. Enjoy this delicious chicken dish that is easy, fast and delicious!

Make delicious Italian Chicken Skillet with Sun-Dried Tomatoes in no time! This delicious one-pan meal combines rosemary, garlic, onion, sun dried tomatoes and spinach for a flavorful dinner the whole family will love. Make it dairy-free by swapping out the heavy cream for a can of coconut cream or homemade cashew cream and topping with nutritional yeast instead of cheese. Ready in under 30 minutes, this delicious Italian Chicken Skillet with Sun Dried Tomatoes will become a regular at your dinner table! Enjoy!

Spinach & Tuna Pancakes

Ingredients

2 tsp rapeseed oil.
2 garlic cloves, chopped.
250g baby spinach.
1 tbsp tomato purée.
120g can tuna steak in spring water, drained.
200g cottage cheese.
2 large eggs.
4 tbsp plain wholemeal flour.

These delicious spinach and tuna pancakes are simple to make and packed with flavour. A great way to get kids eating their vegetables!

To make these healthy lunch recipes for kids, you will need: 2 tsp rapeseed oil, 2 garlic cloves chopped, 250g baby spinach, 1 tbsp tomato purée, 120g can tuna steak in spring water, drained, 200g cottage cheese, 2 large eggs and 4 tbsp plain wholemeal flour.

First heat the oil in a medium-sized pan set over a low heat. Add the garlic and cook for 1 minute until lightly golden; then add the spinach and tomato purée and cook, stirring often, for 3 minutes until the spinach has wilted. Add the tuna and cottage cheese to the pan and stir everything together; then season with some salt and pepper.

In a separate bowl, whisk together the eggs and flour until smooth. Pour this over the ingredients in the pan, stirring them together carefully with a wooden spoon. When everything is combined, turn up the heat to medium and cook, stirring occasionally, until the mixture thickens slightly.

Divide the pancakes into 4-5 portions and spoon into a plate. Serve with a salad or vegetables of your choice for an easy and healthy lunch recipe that kids will love! Enjoy!

Arugula Pizza

1 ¼ cup pizza sauce (purchased or our favorite Easy Pizza Sauce)
1 cup (3 ounces) shredded smoked gouda cheese.
½ cup shredded Parmesan cheese.
6 ounces fresh mozzarella cheese.
4 cups (3 ounces) baby arugula.
1 tablespoon extra virgin olive oil.
¼ teaspoon kosher salt, plus more for sprinkling.

If you're looking for delicious pizza recipes, look no further than this delicious arugula pizza. This delicious and easy-to-prepare meal is perfect for any day of the week. To make it, start by preheating your oven to 500°F (260°C). Next, spread 1 ¼ cups of purchased or homemade pizza sauce on a 12 inch baking sheet lined with parchment paper. Top with 1 cup (3 ounces) shredded smoked gouda cheese, ½ cup shredded Parmesan cheese, and 6 ounces fresh mozzarella cheese. Bake in the preheated oven for 10 minutes until golden brown and bubbly. Once done baking, top the pizza with 4 cups (3 ounces) baby arugula and sprinkle with 1 tablespoon extra virgin olive oil and ¼ teaspoon kosher salt. Slice, serve, and enjoy! With its delicious combination of flavors, this delicious arugula pizza is sure to become a family favorite. Enjoy!

Chicken Cacciatore

Chicken Cacciatore is an easy and fast chicken recipe that can be prepared in no time. It's a hearty yet healthy Italian dish made with bone-in, skin-on chicken thighs or you can use deboned breasts, legs, and wings. This dish features a delicious medley of vegetables like yellow onion, garlic, mushrooms, and bell pepper that lend it a variety of flavors. To make the sauce, crushed tomatoes and tomato paste are added together with fresh herbs like rosemary, parsley, and basil for an herbaceous flavor and spicy kick from red pepper flakes and dried oregano. To prepare this easy dish, start by heating some oil in a large pan or dutch oven. Then, add the chicken to cook until it's golden brown on both sides before removing from pan. Add the onions, garlic, mushrooms and bell peppers to the same pan and sauté for a few minutes before adding in the crushed tomatoes and tomato paste. Simmer everything together until mixed well then add in your herbs and spices. Put the chicken back into the pan, cover and cook for about 30 minutes until chicken is cooked through. Serve over pasta or with a side of mashed potatoes and enjoy! With easy to find ingredients, you can make this easy and delicious Chicken Cacciatore dish in no time.
Bon Appétit!

Mushroom Bolognese

Ingredients for Mushroom Bolognese:

2 onions, finely diced
4 large garlic cloves, chopped
2 large carrots, finely diced
2 sticks of celery, finely diced
400g mushrooms (any variety), finely chopped like mince
2 x 400g tins of whole plum tomatoes
Splash of balsamic vinegar
Glass of red wine
Salt and black pepper, to taste
Olive oil, for cooking
400g spaghetti or pasta of choice

Instructions:

Heat a generous amount of olive oil in a large saucepan over medium heat.

Add the onions and garlic, and sauté for 3-4 minutes until softened.

Add the carrots and celery, and sauté for another 5 minutes until the vegetables are slightly softened.

Add the finely chopped mushrooms to the pan, and cook for 10-15 minutes until the mushrooms have released their moisture and have browned.

Pour in the tinned plum tomatoes, using a wooden spoon to break up any large chunks.

Add a splash of balsamic vinegar and a glass of red wine to the pan.

Season with salt and black pepper to taste, and stir everything together.

Bring the sauce to a simmer and let it cook for about 30 minutes until it has thickened and the vegetables are tender.

While the sauce is cooking, cook the spaghetti in a large pot of salted boiling water according to the package instructions.

Once the spaghetti is cooked al dente, reserve a cup of the pasta cooking water and drain the spaghetti.

Add the spaghetti to the pan with the mushroom bolognese sauce and toss to coat the pasta with the sauce. If the sauce seems too thick, add a splash of the reserved pasta cooking water to loosen it up.

Serve the Mushroom Bolognese over the spaghetti, and enjoy!

Baked Feta Pasta

ingredients

2 pints (20 oz) grape tomatoes.
1/2 cup extra-virgin olive oil.
Salt and freshly ground black pepper.
7 oz. block feta cheese (sheep's milk variety), drained.
10 oz. dry pasta (bite size)
5 medium garlic cloves, peeled and halved.
8 oz. ...
1/4 tsp crushed red pepper flakes, or more to taste.

Baked Feta Pasta is an easy and healthy dish that takes only minimal time to prepare. With just a handful of simple ingredients, you can create this delicious meal. To make it, start by preheating your oven to 425 degrees Fahrenheit.

In a large bowl, combine the grape tomatoes, extra-virgin olive oil, salt and pepper. Cut the feta cheese into small cubes and add it to the bowl. Next, cook 10 oz of bite-size pasta according to package instructions until al dente. Once done, drain it and mix it with the tomato mixture in the bowl.

Add garlic cloves, 8 oz of mushrooms (sliced), and 1/4 tsp of crushed red pepper flakes, or to taste. Toss everything together and spread it in a single layer on an oven-safe dish. Bake for 25 minutes until the top is lightly golden brown.

Baked Feta Pasta is now ready to enjoy! Serve with a sprinkling of fresh herbs, extra olive oil, and a side of crusty bread. This healthy pasta dish makes for a great weeknight dinner that is sure to please the whole family.
Enjoy!

Chicken Enchilada Casserole

This easy and fast Chicken Enchilada Casserole is a great weeknight meal option. With just 5 simple ingredients - chicken, tortillas, beans, cheese and enchilada sauce - you can have this delicious dish on the table in no time.

To prepare the casserole, simply layer the chicken, tortillas, beans and cheese in a casserole dish. Top with enchilada sauce and bake until golden brown.

Serve with a side of sour cream and chopped tomatoes for a complete meal. This easy chicken recipe is sure to become one of your favorite weeknight meals! Enjoy!

Tofu Sandwich

Are you looking for vegetarian recipes for kids? Then look no further than this delicious tofu sandwich. It's a healthy and easy meal that your children will adore. Start by toasting some of their favorite bread, and spread with Thousand Island dressing. To make the sandwich extra special, add lettuce, tomatoes, avocado, cucumber and sprouts. This vegetarian recipe is sure to please everyone in the family! To prepare it, simply assemble all of the ingredients into the sandwich and serve. Your kids will love it! Enjoy!

The tofu sandwich is a great vegetarian alternative for kids and makes a healthy, easy meal that can be prepared quickly. A delicious combination of toasted bread, Thousand Island dressing, lettuce, tomatoes, avocado, cucumber and sprouts makes this vegetarian recipe both nutritious and tasty. It's an ideal way to get your kids to enjoy vegetarian meals - just assemble the ingredients into the sandwich and serve! Your children will love it and you can feel good knowing they are getting their daily dose of veggies. Kids need all the nutrition they can get - so why not try this vegetarian recipe today? Enjoy!

Mac And Cheese

Ingredients

8 ounces uncooked elbow macaroni.
¼ cup salted butter.
3 tablespoons all-purpose flour. Great Value All-Purpose Flour, 5LB. ...
2 ½ cups milk, or more as needed.
2 cups shredded sharp Cheddar cheese.
½ cup finely grated Parmesan cheese. ...
salt and ground black pepper to taste (Optional)

Making macaroni and cheese is a healthy and easy dinner for kids, as it is an excellent source of calcium and protein. With the right ingredients, you can make this classic dish in minutes.

To get started, bring a large pot of salted water to a boil over high heat. Add 8 ounces of uncooked elbow macaroni, and cook until al dente (about 7 minutes). Drain the cooked pasta in a colander.

Meanwhile, melt ¼ cup of salted butter in a large saucepan over medium heat. Add 3 tablespoons of all-purpose flour to the melted butter, stirring constantly until the mixture thickens slightly and becomes a paste. Slowly add 2 ½ cups of milk to the saucepan, continually stirring until fully incorporated and thickened.

Remove the pan from heat and stir in 2 cups of shredded sharp Cheddar cheese, ½ cup of finely grated Parmesan cheese, and salt and ground black pepper to taste (optional). Add the cooked macaroni to the saucepan and mix until all of the pasta is evenly coated.

Serve the macaroni and cheese hot, with extra Parmesan cheese sprinkled on top if desired. Enjoy!

Creamy Tomato Soup

Tomato Soup is a great lunch choice for kids because it's easy to make and packed with healthy ingredients. Plus, they will love the bright and vibrant colour! Here's what you'll need to make this delicious tomato soup recipe:

- 1-1.25kg/2lb 4oz-2lb 12oz ripe tomatoes
- 1 medium onion
- 1 small carrot
- 1 celery stick
- 2 tbsp olive oil
- 2 squirts of tomato purée (about 2 tsp)
- A good pinch of sugar
- 2 bay leaves

Once you've gathered all the ingredients, it's time to start cooking! Begin by heating the olive oil in a large saucepan and adding the diced onion, carrot, celery stick. Cook over medium heat for about 5 minutes until softened. Then add the tomatoes, purée, bay leaves and sugar. Cover with a lid and cook for 40 minutes. Once the soup is cooked, remove the bay leaves and blend until smooth with a blender.

Serve up this delicious tomato soup with some crusty bread or croutons on top and you have an easy, healthy lunch that your kids will love! Enjoy!

Chicken Quesadillas

Ingredients

1 pound skinless, boneless chicken breast, diced.
1 (1.27 ounce) packet fajita seasoning.
1 tablespoon vegetable oil.
2 green bell peppers, chopped.
2 red bell peppers, chopped.
1 onion, chopped. ...
10 (10 inch) flour tortillas.
1 (8 ounce) package shredded Cheddar cheese.

Chicken quesadillas make for a healthy and easy dinner for the whole family. To start preparing, dice the boneless chicken breasts and season with fajita seasoning. In a large skillet over medium heat, heat vegetable oil and add in the diced chicken breast, green bell peppers, red bell peppers, and onions. Cook until vegetables are softened and chicken is cooked through. To assemble the quesadillas, place about ¼ cup of cheese onto one side of a tortilla. Top with cooked vegetables and chicken, then add another ¼ cup of cheese to the top. Fold over into a half-moon shape and cook in a skillet on medium-high heat until golden brown. Repeat this process with the remaining tortillas. Serve warm and enjoy!

For a fun variation, try adding black beans to the quesadillas or swapping out Cheddar cheese for Monterey Jack. Using flavorful ingredients like jalapenos, salsa, and guacamole can also liven up this classic dish. Chicken quesadillas make for a healthy and delicious dinner that can be customized to fit the tastes of any family. Enjoy!

Chicken Noodle Casserole

Ingredients
12 oz. wide egg noodles.
10.5-oz. cans cream of chicken soup.
1 c. whole milk.
1 c. shredded sharp cheddar cheese.
1 tsp. ground black pepper.
1/2 tsp. kosher salt.
3 c. cooked, shredded chicken (from 1 rotisserie chicken)
1/2. small yellow onion, finely chopped.

Making a chicken noodle casserole is an easy and healthy dinner option for kids. To begin, preheat your oven to 400 degrees Fahrenheit. In a large pot over medium heat, cook the egg noodles according to package directions. Drain the cooked noodles and set aside.

In a medium-sized bowl, combine the cream of chicken soup, milk, shredded cheese, ground black pepper and kosher salt. Stir until the ingredients are completely blended.

In a 9-by-13-inch baking dish, spread the cooked egg noodles. Top with the shredded chicken and onion pieces. Pour the cream of chicken mixture over the noodles and chicken, spreading evenly to ensure everything is coated.

Bake for 25 minutes until the cheese is melted and bubbly. Let cool for about 10 minutes before serving. Enjoy!

This chicken noodle casserole provides a comforting, delicious and healthy dinner option for kids. It's quick to prepare, full of flavor and sure to please everyone at the table.

Lemon Mushroom Chicken

Ingredients:

4 chicken breasts (about 3/4 pound total)
1 1/2 tbsp unsalted butter, divided
8 oz cremini mushrooms, sliced
1/4 tsp salt
1/2 cup dry sherry
1/4 cup lemon juice
1/2 cup heavy cream
2 1/2 cups baby spinach

Instructions:

Season the chicken breasts with salt and pepper.

In a large pan, heat 1 tbsp of butter over medium heat. Add the chicken breasts and cook for about 4-5 minutes on each side, or until golden brown and fully cooked. Remove the chicken from the pan and set aside.

In the same pan, add the remaining butter and sliced mushrooms. Cook the mushrooms for about 4-5 minutes, or until they are tender and lightly browned.

Add the sherry to the pan and use a wooden spoon to scrape the bottom of the pan to release any browned bits. Cook the sherry for about 2 minutes, or until it has reduced by half.

Add the lemon juice and heavy cream to the pan and stir to combine. Cook the sauce for about 2-3 minutes, or until it has thickened slightly.

Return the chicken breasts to the pan and add the baby spinach. Stir to combine and cook for about 2 minutes, or until the spinach has wilted.

Serve the chicken with the lemon mushroom sauce on top. Enjoy!

Broccoli Shrimp Alfredo

Ingredients

1 16-ounce packages fettuccine.
1 pound uncooked medium shrimp, peeled and deveined.
3 garlic cloves, minced.
½ cup butter, cubed.
1 8-ounce packages cream cheese, cubed.
1 cup milk.
½ cup shredded Parmesan cheese.
6 cups frozen broccoli florets.

Instructions:

Cook the fettuccine according to the package instructions until al dente. Drain and set aside.

In a large skillet or saucepan, heat some oil over medium heat. Add the minced garlic and cook for 30 seconds until fragrant.

Add the uncooked shrimp to the skillet and cook until pink and cooked through, about 2-3 minutes. Remove the shrimp from the skillet and set aside.

In the same skillet, melt the butter over medium heat. Stir in the cream cheese until melted and smooth.

Gradually add the milk to the skillet, whisking constantly, until the sauce is smooth and creamy. Stir in the shredded Parmesan cheese until melted and well combined.

Stir in the cooked fettuccine, cooked shrimp, and frozen broccoli florets into the sauce until well combined.

Cook the broccoli shrimp alfredo until the broccoli is tender and heated through, about 3-5 minutes.

Serve the broccoli shrimp alfredo hot, garnished with additional Parmesan cheese and fresh herbs if desired.

Enjoy your delicious and creamy broccoli shrimp alfredo!

Grilled Hot Dogs

Grilled hot dogs are a classic summer cookout favorite. They're also an easy and healthy dinner option for kids. Preparing grilled hot dogs is super simple - all you need to do is gather the ingredients, heat up your grill, and get cooking!

To prepare grilled hot dogs, you'll need eight hot dogs, ¼ cup ketchup, 2 Tbsp Worcestershire Sauce, 1 minced garlic clove, and 1 tsp of vegetable oil. Start by preheating the grill to medium-high heat. Once it's hot enough, place the hot dogs on the grill and cook for about 8 minutes or until browned and cooked through.

In a small bowl, mix together the ketchup, Worcestershire sauce, garlic and vegetable oil. Brush the hot dogs with the mixture when they come off of the grill. Serve with your favorite condiments and sides for a delicious summer meal! Enjoy!

Baked Rigatoni Pasta

Ingredients

1 pound rigatoni.
1 pound ground Italian sausage.
1 pound 90/10 ground beef.
1 cup diced yellow onion.
4 garlic cloves, minced.
1 (24 ounce) jar marinara sauce or homemade.
1 (24 ounce) can crushed tomatoes.
1 teaspoon kosher salt.

If you're looking for a healthy and hearty pasta dish, look no further than baked rigatoni! This delicious meal is loaded with healthy ingredients like Italian sausage, ground beef, diced onion, garlic and marinara sauce. Plus it comes together in just one pot for easy preparation. Here's how to make this tasty dish:

Begin by preheating the oven to 350°F. Then, bring a large pot of salted water to a boil and add 1 pound of rigatoni. Cook for 8-10 minutes, stirring occasionally until al dente. Drain and set aside.

In a large skillet over medium-high heat, brown the Italian sausage and ground beef until fully cooked, stirring occasionally. Add the diced yellow onion and minced garlic and sauté until softened, about 3-4 minutes.

Transfer the meat mixture to a large baking dish, then add in the marinara sauce/homemade sauce, crushed tomatoes and salt. Stir everything together. Add the drained rigatoni and stir everything together to evenly coat in the sauce.

Cover the dish with aluminum foil and bake for 20 minutes or until bubbling. Remove from oven and let cool for a few minutes before serving. Enjoy!

Potato Soup

Ingredients

8 slices thin bacon, cut into 1-inch pieces
1 medium onion, diced
2 medium carrots, scrubbed clean and diced
2 stalks celery, diced
4 small russet potatoes, peeled and diced
8 cups low-sodium chicken or vegetable broth
3 tablespoons all-purpose flour
1 cup milk

Instructions for preparing Potato Soup:

In a large pot, cook the bacon over medium heat until crispy, about 5-7 minutes. Remove the bacon with a slotted spoon and set aside. Reserve 2 tablespoons of the bacon fat in the pot.

Add the diced onion, carrots, and celery to the pot and cook until the vegetables are soft and the onion is translucent, about 5-7 minutes.

Stir in the diced potatoes and the chicken or vegetable broth. Bring the soup to a boil, then reduce the heat and simmer until the potatoes are tender, about 20-25 minutes.

In a separate bowl, whisk together the flour and milk until smooth. Stir the flour mixture into the soup and cook until the soup has thickened, about 5-7 minutes.

Return the cooked bacon to the pot and stir to combine. Season the soup with salt and pepper, to taste.

Serve the soup hot, garnished with freshly chopped parsley or green onions, if desired.

Enjoy your delicious and comforting Potato Soup!

Baked Fish

Here's a list of ingredients for a baked fish recipe:

White fish fillets
Cherry tomatoes
Red onion
Garlic
Green olives
Capers
Fresh parsley
Olive oil
Dried oregano
Lemon juice
Salt and pepper, to taste

Instructions:

Preheat the oven to 375°F (190°C).

Line a baking dish with parchment paper or lightly grease it with oil.

Rinse the fish fillets and pat them dry with paper towels. Place them in the prepared baking dish.

Slice the cherry tomatoes in half and arrange them around the fish fillets.

Thinly slice the red onion and scatter it over the tomatoes.

Mince the garlic and sprinkle it over the onions.

Add the green olives and capers to the dish.

Chop the fresh parsley and sprinkle it over the top of the fish.

Drizzle the dish with olive oil and sprinkle with dried oregano.

Squeeze the lemon juice over the dish and season with salt and pepper, to taste.

Bake the fish in the preheated oven for 20-25 minutes, or until the fish is opaque and flakes easily with a fork.

Serve the baked fish hot, garnished with additional chopped parsley, if desired. Enjoy!

Meatballs Spaghetti

Meatball spaghetti is a delicious and easy-to-make recipe for kids. This delicious dish is made with spaghetti noodles, ground beef, bread crumbs, parsley, Parmesan cheese, egg, garlic cloves, salt, red pepper flakes, extra-virgin olive oil, onion chopped finely, crushed tomatoes and one bay leaf.

To begin, cook the spaghetti noodles according to package instructions. While the pasta is cooking, prepare the meatballs: In a large bowl combine ground beef, bread crumbs, parsley, Parmesan cheese, egg and garlic cloves. Using your hands or a wooden spoon mix until everything is combined. Form into small balls about 1 inch in diameter, and set aside.

Heat a large skillet over medium heat and add the olive oil. Add the meatballs to the pan and cook until golden brown all over, about 5 minutes. Remove from the heat and set aside.

Add the onion to the same skillet over medium-high heat and sauté for 3 minutes. Add the crushed tomatoes, bay leaf and red pepper flakes and season with salt and pepper to taste. Bring to a simmer and add the cooked meatballs back into the sauce. Simmer for about 10 minutes until sauce has thickened.

Once spaghetti is done cooking, drain it and toss it in the skillet with the meatballs and sauce. Mix everything together and serve with freshly grated Parmesan cheese on top. Enjoy!

Meatball spaghetti is a delicious dish that can be enjoyed by the whole family. With its delicious combination of ingredients, it's sure to be a hit in any household! Try this delicious recipe today and enjoy delicious Italian-style food with your family and friends. Buon Appetito!

Chicken Burger

Making easy and fast chicken burgers is a great way to enjoy a tasty meal. These easy-to-prepare chicken burgers are made with only a few simple ingredients. To begin, combine the ground chicken breast, minced garlic, chopped chives, chopped oregano, lemon juice, breadcrumbs, mayo, salt and pepper in a large bowl. Mix the ingredients until they are thoroughly combined and form into patties.

Heat a skillet over medium heat and cook the chicken burgers for about 4-5 minutes on each side, or until cooked through. Serve these delicious chicken burgers with your favorite toppings such as lettuce, tomato, onion, cheese and pickles. Enjoy your easy and fast chicken burgers!

Making easy and fast chicken recipes doesn't have to be complicated when you follow this easy recipe. With just a few simple ingredients, you can enjoy delicious homemade chicken burgers that are sure to please the whole family. So don't wait - try out these easy and fast chicken burger recipes today!

Buffalo Chicken Wrap

Ingredients

1 pound boneless skinless chicken breasts.
2 Tablespoons olive oil.
1/2 cup Frank's Hot Sauce.
1/2 teaspoon paprika.
1/2 teaspoon garlic powder.
pinch of salt.
4 large flour tortillas.
1/2 cup Blue cheese or Ranch dressing.

For easy and fast chicken recipes, a buffalo chicken wrap is the perfect go-to dish. It's easy to prepare and only requires a handful of simple ingredients. Start by marinating the chicken breasts in olive oil, hot sauce, paprika, garlic powder and salt for at least 30 minutes. Then heat up a skillet over medium-high heat and cook the chicken for about 10 minutes or until cooked through. Once it's cooked, chop up the chicken then warm up four large tortillas in a dry skillet. Spread equal amounts of dressing over each wrap, top off with some chopped chicken then carefully roll them up. For an extra kick of flavor, add some extra hot sauce to your wrap. Enjoy your easy and fast buffalo chicken wrap!

Mushroom Pasta With Parmesan

Ingredients

8 ounces* short pasta, like penne, rigatoni, or casarecce, plus saved pasta water.
16 ounces baby bella (cremini) mushrooms (or a mix of other types)
1/2 small sweet onion or yellow onion.
4 tablespoons olive oil, divided.
¾ teaspoon kosher salt, divided.
3 tablespoons salted butter, divided.

This healthy mushroom pasta with parmesan is a quick and easy meal that can be made in 30 minutes or less! To prepare this dish, begin by boiling the 8 ounces of short pasta until al dente. Reserve some of the pasta water to use later when making your sauce. While the pasta cooks, heat 2 tablespoons of olive oil in a large skillet. Add in the mushrooms and onion, and season with 1/2 teaspoon of salt. Cook until the vegetables are softened and lightly browned, about 8-10 minutes. Remove from heat and set aside.

In a separate pan, melt 2 tablespoons of butter over medium heat. Once melted, add in the remaining 2 tablespoons of olive oil, and the cooked vegetables. Give everything a good stir to combine. Continue cooking for another 5 minutes or so until the sauce is golden and bubbly. Add in the reserved pasta water, 1/4 teaspoon of kosher salt, and freshly grated parmesan cheese (to taste). Stir to combine, then add in the cooked pasta. Give everything a good stir before serving! Enjoy your healthy mushroom pasta with parmesan hot, topped with extra parmesan cheese and freshly chopped parsley if desired. Bon Appétit!

Avocado Fusilli Pasta

Ingredients

350g fusilli.
2 cloves garlic, peeled.
200g baby spinach.
2 small ripe avocados, halved and stoned.
extra-virgin olive oil, for drizzling.
30g roasted cashews, chopped.
30g roasted almonds, chopped.
a small bunch coriander, chopped.

For healthy and delicious pasta, you can't go wrong with this avocado fusilli recipe! Start by bringing a large pot of salted water to the boil. Add the fusilli and cook until al dente. Meanwhile, in a large pan over medium heat, add some olive oil and garlic cloves. Saute for 5 minutes until fragrant. Add the baby spinach and cook for a few minutes until wilted. When the pasta is cooked, drain it and add to the pan with the spinach mixture. Finally, top with halved avocados, roasted cashews and almonds and chopped coriander. Drizzle with some extra-virgin olive oil for a healthy finish. Serve and enjoy! This healthy pasta dish is sure to become a favorite in your house. With its creamy avocado, crunchy nuts, and delicious flavors from the garlic, spinach and coriander, it's an easy healthy meal that everyone can enjoy. Try this avocado fusilli recipe today!

I want to take a moment to express my heartfelt gratitude for your recent purchase of my recipe book. As a passionate food lover, nothing makes me happier than sharing my favorite recipes with others. Your decision to invest in my book not only supports my dream, but also shows your commitment to expanding your culinary horizons.

I sincerely hope that the recipes in the book will inspire you to try new things and add some excitement to your meals.

Thank you again for your support and for being a part of this journey with me. I hope my book will bring you many happy and delicious moments in the kitchen.

www.ingramcontent.com/pod-product-compliance
Lightning Source LLC
Chambersburg PA
CBHW041151110526
44590CB00027B/4191